Mir

Translation of Mir Taqi Mir's popular Urdu couplets

Swati Sani

Dedicated to my father

Girish Kumar Shrivastava

Contents

Thank you vii

Proem ix

Urdu Poetry, A Timeline 1

   Evolution of Urdu Poetry 3

   The Golden Era 5

Urdu Poetry and Literary Movements 9

   Classiki Adab (The Classical Literature) 9

   Aligarh Tahreek (The Aligarh Movement) 11

   Roomaniyat Ki Tahreek (Romanticism) 12

   Taraqqui-Pasand Tahreek (The Progressive Writers' Movement) 12

   Halqa-e-Arbab-e-Zauq (The Circle of Connoisseurs) 14

   Jadidiyat (The Modernist Movement) 15

   Maa-ba'd Jadidiyat (Post-Modernism) 17

Mir Taqi Mir 19

Intekhab 27

Forms and structure of Urdu poetry 79

Thank you

Janab Hamid Iqbal Siddiqui Saheb, for encouraging, guiding, and giving me the confidence to embark on this project.

Deepshikha Seth, for reading every word I wrote, right from the very first draft of the book, and for editing this work.

Shubnam Gill, for allowing me to use a picture of the beautiful painting of Mir Taqi Mir that she has made.

Dr. Tarique Sani, my husband, who motivated me to bring out the print edition of the book series for my readers.

Proem

Everyone loves the quotability of Urdu poetry. From the people at the seat of power to lovers, in everyday conversations to board meetings, and even in the court of law, one often finds Urdu couplets being quoted.

While it is easy to pick up a dictionary and decipher the meaning of individual words, the poems often have a social, historical, and political perspective since Urdu poetry has evolved and progressed through its various literary movements (*tahreek*).

Mir is the second book in a series of eight books, wherein I have tried to present an easy way to understand Urdu poetry in the light of these literary movements. The books will cover the examples of couplets from the traditional writing styles to the modern and postmodern periods.

Mir Taqi Mir's poetry is easy to understand but tough to translate in another language in a way that it brings out exactly what the poet wanted to convey. He is an expert craftsman, the God of poetry, and we, mere mortals, struggle to understand the insights his writings present.

I have chosen 50 popular couplets from the works of Mir, and have attempted to lyrically translate them into English. The original couplets are presented in Urdu, Devanagari, and Roman scripts.

The book also has sections on the timeline of Urdu poetry, and major literary movements of Urdu poetry. Both of these are vast and fairly complicated topics, but I have tried to simplify and present them in brief, and as per my understanding.

I have tried to be thorough, but it is possible that there may be some omissions or errors. I hope the reader would excuse me for this, and point them out to me so that corrections can be made in future editions.

Swati Sani

17th November, 2022

x

Urdu Poetry, A Timeline

Urdu, a language so enchanting and beautiful that you cannot help but fall in love with it — exuding love, romance, culture, sophistication, and spirituality all at once. A tall claim for a language so young, just about a few centuries old, but as Daagh Dehlvi rightly claims, the entire Hindustan loves Urdu.

Urdu hai jis ka naam hameeN jaante haiN 'Daagh'
Hindostan meiN dhoom hamari ZabaN ki hai
(Daagh Dehlvi)

The language that is Urdu, only we know 'Daagh'and how
the entire Hindostan speaks and celebrates it now.

History often sounds dull, boring, and academic, but not when it is about a language that evolved over several centuries — a language that continues to evolve even today.

It all began with the ingress of invaders to northern India sometime around the 12th century. While the kings built their kingdoms, the soldiers and mercenaries who came along mingled with the populace. They spoke Arabic, Persian, Turkish, and a few other languages, and a large number of them decided to settle down in the newly conquered lands.

These soldiers interacted by intermingling the words of their language with that of the locals. This intermingling of Hindu and Muslim cultures during the Islamic conquests gave birth to a composite culture, the *Ganga-Jamuni tahzeeb*, and a new language.

Over time, what initially began as a dialect developed into a full-fledged language that derived its words from Indo-Aryan and Iranian languages. While its basic grammar structure was based on *khadi boli*, the writers used Persian script to formalize it because Persian was the official language of the Mughal court. This new language, as it evolved, was known by several names.

Shakespeare has famously said, 'what's in a name?'. But this does not seem to hold true when we talk of Urdu. Its name changed based on the region where it was spoken. The earliest English writers called it Moors. The famous linguist, Dr. John Gilchrist, coined the word Hindustani in about 1787 AD and made it official. Dehlvi, Hindi and Hindawi were used by older writers of the age of Mir and Mushafi as a distinction from Persian and to show that the language is a product of Hindustan. The people of Deccan called their dialect of Urdu as Dakhni.

Mughal emperor Shahjahan referred to the language as Urdu-e-mua'lla, whereas some scholars adopted the term Rekhta. It is not clear, but it is said that the term Rekhta was adopted for the 'literary expression' to differentiate it from the 'vernacular dialect'.

However, even before the formal usage of the word Urdu, there are evidences of its usage during the period of Mongol king Changez Khan (1162-1227). Changez Khan's army was divided into four units: the royal camp called *Urdu-e-mutalla* (the golden camp), the camp of royal princes called *Urdu-e-muzhab* (the silver camp), the camp for nobles called *Urdu-e-mu'alla* (the exalted camp) and the camp for rank and file was simply called *Urdu*. The last two terms for these army camps were the names given to this new language because the members of these camps intermingled and communicated with the ordinary folks, giving birth to a new language. The name Urdu was first used by Mushafi Ghulam Hamdani around 1780. The word is derived from the Turkish word Oordu, meaning a camp or an army.

Evolution of Urdu Poetry

Unlike the evolutionary journey of English poetry, Urdu poetry did not pass through the slow process of grinding, which is very invigorating and healthy for a budding language. The themes, imagery, and rhythmic patterns of the earliest Urdu poetry were borrowed from Persian literature. In fact, several initial Urdu verses were literal translations of Persian poetry, restricting it to the elite class.

In the 13th century, the first poet of the Urdu language, Amir Khusrau, composed couplets with one *misra* (line of the couplet) in Persian and the second in the local dialect *khari boli* which appealed to the sensibilities of the common folk. Here is a *sher* from the very first ghazal written in Rekhta by Amir Khusrau:

Shabaan-e-hijraN darraz chuN zulf o roz-e- vaslat chuN umr kotaah
sakhi piya ko jo maiN na dekhuN to kaise kaatuN andheri ratiyaN
(Amir Khusrau)

The long night of separations are like long manes;
and the days of the union as short as life itself
my friend, without looking at the face of my beloved,
how will I pass these long nights of separation

Amir Khusrau went on to compose doha, paheli, kah-mukri, qawallis, and other poetic forms in the local dialect Hindawi, that derived words from the north Indian languages as well as from Arabic, Persian, and Turkish.

Apart from Amir Khusrau, Saint Banda Nawas Gesu Daraz (1321-1442), Sant Kabirdas (1398-1518), and Meerabai (1498-1547) also composed their poems in Hindawi.

In the 16th century, Mohammad Quli Qutub Shah (1565-1612), the fifth Sultan of the Qutub Shahi dynasty of Golconda was also a poet, who wrote in Persian, Telugu, and Hindawi.

He is the first Urdu poet to have published his poetry collection (a *Diwan*), making him the first *Sahib-e-Diwan* of Urdu Literature.

The Sultan was a man in love, and most of his poetry is romantic as is evident from one of his verses:

> *Kahii thii piya bin suburi karuN*
> *kahaya jaaye amma kiya jaaye na*
> *(Quli Qutub Shah)*

> *I was told to have patience; when I missed you, my beloved*
> *so easy for you to say it, but so hard for me to be without my beloved*

Wali Mohammad Wali, also called Wali Dakini (1667-1707), is said to be the first poet to have composed *ghazals* in thought and form that reflected the language spoken by the common folk:

> *Kiya mujh ishq ne zalim kuN aab aahista*
> *ki aatish gul ko karti hai gulaab aahista*
> *(Wali Dakini)*

> *She is cruel, but my love has melted her bit by bit*
> *like the fire that extracts the essence of rose bit by bit*

Wali Dakini's visit to Delhi sometime in the 1700s, along with his Divan of *ghazals*, made stalwarts of the literary circles notice his unique style of poetry, which was non-Persianised as opposed to the Persianised style being used by the poets of that era. His poetry not just created a ripple at that time, but it also inspired the future generations of poets like Zauk, Sauda, and Mir to write colloquial poetry with local themes, imagery, and idioms. This was the turning point for Urdu — which by then had come to be known as Rekhta. Urdu *ghazal* took form and shape around this time. Inspired by Wali Dakini, Mir Taqi Mir has said:

> *Khugar nahiN kuchh yuN hi ham rekhta goii ke*
> *maashuuq jo tha apna banda-e-Dakan tha*
> *(Mir Taqi Mir)*

> *It is not by chance that I am addicted to talking in Rekhta*
> *The one who was my love was a native of Deccan*

The regular people on the street had by then begun to converse in Urdu. Urdu poetry, too, had evolved into a personal mode of communication and social engagement. The courtesans of Delhi took to the Urdu ghazal and enriched it further. Referring to them, Mushafi writes:

> *Aye Mushafi tu in se mohabbat na kijiyo*
> *zaalim ghazab ki hoti haiN ye dilli-waliyaN*
> *(Mushafi Ghulam Hamdani)*

> *Do not fall in love, o Mushafi, with them*
> *you know how very ruthless the Delhi women are*

The Golden Era

During the 18th and 19th centuries, India was riddled with invasions and devastation. Delhi was repeatedly looted and destroyed by multiple invasions by Afghans and Marathas. The looming desolation forced many people, including artists and litterateurs, to migrate from the city and the court culture that prevailed during the Mughal era saw a decline.

Dilli hui hai veeraN soone khandar pade haiN
veeran haiN mohalle sunsaan ghar pade haiN
(Mushafi Ghulam Hamdani)

Delhi has become desolate, and the ruins are lonely
the mohallas are deserted, and homes are empty

However, every time after destruction, whenever the city was inhabited again, its splendour not only returned but grew manifold.

This was also the period when Urdu poetry reached the highest degree of artistic and literary brilliance.

Laayi haayat aayi qazaa le chali chale
apni khushi na aaye, na apni khushi chale
(Sheikh Ibrahim Zauk)

When life ordained, I was born; when death commands, I will move on
I did not come of my own accord, and my willingness won't count for me
to be gone

Bahadur Shah Zafar was a connoisseur, and himself a gifted poet. He regularly held and presided over *mushairas* in his court and invited well-known Urdu poets, such as Sheikh Ibrahim Zauk, Momin Khan Momin, Daagh Dehlvi, Nawab Mustafa Khan Shefta, and Mirza Ghalib, among others.

Though the country was entirely under the influence of the British in the mid-19th century, and the emperor was just a figurehead, these *mushairas* and *mehfils* continued. The uncertainties that riddled the country after the 1857 Sepoy Mutiny left the social and cultural milieu of the country floundering for a while. This also gets reflected in the literature written around that time.

When the last Mughal Emperor, Bahadur Shah Zafar, was exiled to Rangoon (Burma), this is what he had to say:

Ay vaa'e inqalaab zamane ke jaur se
Dilli 'Zafar' ke haath se pal meiN nikal gayi
(Bahadur Shah Zafar)

Ah! The revolution and the cruelty of times
Delhi has slipped out of 'Zafar's' hand in an instant

Other poets too mourned the lost glories of the Mughal era as the events of the mutiny left an indelible mark on the Indian social and cultural scene, and the poetry reflected a deep melancholy:

Jab ki tujh bin nahi koi maujood
phir ye hangama ai khudaa kya hai
(Mirza Ghalib)

You are omnipresent; there is no doubt
Almighty! then what is this uproar all about

In short, while Urdu poetry originated in melancholic romance, a subject borrowed from Persian literature, it flourished and was firmly established in the Mughal era as the poets experimented with language, similes, and imagery, giving it a very local Hindustani flavour.

Urdu Poetry and Literary Movements

To understand any poetry, it is often essential to know the context it was written in. Literary movements provide this much-needed context.

All works of literature, poetry included, reflect the times they were written in, help readers learn about the poet, and give insight into the lives of common folk. Literary movements are broad periods that share common themes and trends in literature.

This article is a very brief outline of Urdu literary movements and their influence on poetry.

Classiki Adab
(The Classical Literature)

The language, tropes, allegories, and analogies used in Amir Khusrau's poetry give us a glimpse of the multi-hued culture, the *Ganga-Jamni tahzeeb* of the 13th and 14th centuries.

> *Jab yaar dekha nain bhar dil ki gayi chinta utar*
> *aisa nahi koi ajab rakhe use samjhaye kar*
> *(Amir Khusrau)*

A loving glance from a beloved and all the anxieties disappeared
there is no one so extraordinary who can keep him pacified

The *sufi kalam* of the pioneer of Urdu poetry, Amir Khusrau, is timeless and is celebrated even today.

Classical Urdu poetry of the 17th and 18th centuries is primarily love poetry and borrowed its structure and form from Persian literature. It also acquired themes, figures of speech and symbolism from Persian ghazals.

> *Jaan ham tujh pe diya karte haiN*
> *naam tera hi liya karte haiN*
> *(Imam Bakhsh Nasikh)*

> *My life is devoted to you*
> *all I do is call out to you*

In the late 18th and early 19th centuries, the works of poets like Insha Ullah Khan Insha, Mir Taqi Mir, and Nazeer Akbarabadi greatly impacted Urdu poetry.

Mir, unlike some of his contemporaries, preferred a language free of flowery Persian words. His poetry was intended for the common man, not for royalty. He proclaims:

> *Sher mere hain sab khawas pasand*
> *par mujhe guftagu aawam se hai*
> *(Mir Taqi Mir)*

> *The distinguished find my poetry appealing*
> *but it is for the common man that I prefer writing*

Nazeer Akbarabadi, too, experimented with various forms of Urdu poetry. While his contemporaries wrote the classical ghazal, he opened new avenues by writing *nazms* and *geet* about the Indian culture and Hindustani traditions. He wrote about the lives and events of the common man, religious festivals, carnivals, sports, hobbies, everything found a place in the poetry of Nazeer. He was the pioneer of the new school of poetry that Hali, Azad and their contemporaries later advocated.

Kya mandir, masjid, taal, kuwaN, kya kheti-baadi, phool, chaman
sab thaath padaa rah jawega jab laad chalega banjara
(Nazir Akbarabadi, nazm: Banjara-nama)

Mosque, temple, lakes and well, farmland flowers, and garden
will be no good when the traveling merchant leaves, packing his goods

The 19th-century classical poets Ghalib, Momin, Zauq, Zafar, and others had a profound influence, and Urdu poetry blossomed considerably during this golden era. While all of the poetic works of this period are outstanding, Ghalib's poetry towers above all others.

Raat din gardish meiN haiN saat aasman
ho rahega kuch na kuch ghabraayeN kya
(Mirza Ghalib)

Day and night, the seven skies wander about
why should I worry? Something will work out

Aligarh Tahreek
(The Aligarh Movement)

After the Sepoy Mutiny of 1857, Sir Syed Ahmed Khan (1817-1898), a social reformer, educationist, and philosopher, started a new socio-religious movement called Aligarh movement. This movement in poetry is known for disassociating with the old style of expression used by classical poets by instituting a simple way of writing with an emphasis on reformist thoughts and moral values.

Farishte se badh kar hai insaan banna
magar is mein lagti hai mehnat ziyada
(Altaf Hussain Hali)

Better a human being than an angel
but then it takes much more work

The Aligarh movement was a bit rigid and heavily stressed on rationalist, reformist, utilitarian and practical thoughts in literature.

Roomaniyat Ki Tahreek
(Romanticism)

To a certain extent, romanticism in Urdu literature was born as a reaction to Sir Syed's Aligarh Movement.

By the end of the 19th century, the Urdu poets felt restricted by morally upright and preachy poetry and favoured imagination and aesthetics. Emotions, feelings, and passion found a place in poetry again. A significant theme of romanticism is nature and its effect on the poet.

Romantic poetry speaks to the audiences directly in a way that they identify with and experience the emotions expressed by the poet.

> *Tabiyat apni ghabarati hai jab sunsaan raatoN meiN*
> *ham aise meiN tiri yadoN ki chaadar taan lete haiN*
> *(Firaq Gorakhpuri)*
>
> *When lonely nights overwhelm me with anxiety*
> *I wrap myself in your comforting and warm memory*

The Romantic movement, as far as Urdu poetry is concerned, never really ended. New ideas and trends have emerged, but the essence of romanticism continues to enrich Urdu poetry.

Taraqqui-Pasand Tahreek
(The Progressive Writers' Movement)

In 1932, a collection of stories was published in the form of a book called *Angaare* by four young writers of India, which was met with outrage from a group of people and religious figures, resulting in the British rulers of India banning the book. However, the writers were unapologetic and stood by what they wrote. The formation of the

Progressive Writers' Association of India was a direct result of banning this book.

'We will have to change the standards of beauty,' said Munshi Premchand at the first conference of the Progressive Writers Association. The movement dreamt of an ideal society, a just political system, and the abolition of social and economic inequalities. Fighting poverty, social backwardness, and decadent morality became the clarion call for its members.

While the Progressive writers' movement gave a massive impetus to prose, Urdu poetry was already inclined towards this thought even before forming the formal association. Poets like Hali, Iqbal, and Chakbast had already liberated Urdu poetry from classical and romantic cliches and had paved the way for the newer generations.

Dard-e-dil paas-e-wafa jazba-e-imaan hona
aadmiya hai yahi aur yahi insaan hona
(Brij Narayan Chakbast)

A sensitive and loyal heart that has honesty and integrity
is all that is required to be a human being; and to humanity

The progressive movement further widened the horizon of Urdu poetry. Freedom fighters like Ram Prasad Bismil went to the gallows reciting these lines penned by Bismil Azimabadi.

Sarfaroshi ki tamanna ab hamare dil meiN hai
dekhna hai zor kitna baazu-e-qatil meiNhai
(Bismil Azimabadi)

There is a fire and a desire for a revolution in our hearts
we will test the strength in the arms of our executioner

There was a balance between emotions, art, and purpose. Even though this was a time when a lot of poetic work sounded like

slogans, poets like Faiz Ahmad Faiz drew upon sources from world literature and imparted a softness to the poetry that did not require sloganeering.

Ham parvarish-e-lauh-o kalam karte rahenge
jo dil pe guzarti hai rakam karte rahenge
(Faiz Ahmad Faiz)

We will continue to nurture the pen and the paper
and will continue to write about the sufferings of our heart

While the progressive writers stressed political reforms and had a socialist agenda, there was one group of poets that felt left out. They did not identify with the literature of sloganeering.

The progressive movement helped further the cause of Urdu poetry, but it was short-lived.

Halqa-e-Arbab-e-Zauq
(The Circle of Connoisseurs)

A few years after the Progressive writers' movement formed, a new group emerged in 1939, and they called themselves Halqa-e-Arbab-e-Zauk — The circle of connoisseurs. The progressives and Halqa-e-Arbab-e-Zauk were not opposed to each other; they just looked at things and expressed themselves differently.

The progressive movement was driven by forces like social and political ills, while the Halqa-e-Arbab-e-Zauk was inclined towards the feelings and emotions of the common man.

The Halqa considered literature as a work of art that required no testimony. At a time when the progressive movement was sweeping through the nation like a storm, the poetry written by the members of the Halqa movement was like a soft, soothing breeze. The early members of Halqa included celebrated poets like Noon Meem Rashid, Qayyum Nazar, and Meeraji. This group mirrored a traditional mode of western Modernist literature and experimented with new verse forms, which were very different from classical Urdu literature.

Meeraji introduced free verse and is also considered the founder of symbolism in Urdu poetry, expanding the canvas of Urdu poetry. Drawing inspiration from western literature, Sanskrit poetry traditions, and Hindu mythology, Meeraji also experimented with form and thought by introducing folklore, legends, and mythology in his poetry.

Parbat ko ek neela banaya kis ne...doori ne
chaand sitaron se dil ko bharmaya kis ne... doori ne
(Meeraji)

Who made the hills an azure secret ... the distance
what made the stars and the sky an allurement... the distance

The group also welcomed poets who wrote ghazals, the traditional form of Urdu poetry. Several members of the progressive movement also got inspired and joined this group.

Halqa-e-Arbab-e-Zauk influenced the Modernist movement of Urdu poetry significantly.

Jadidiyat
(The Modernist Movement)

The seeds of Modernism were sowed in Urdu poetry in the late 19th century by Altaf Hussain Hali, Mohammad Hussain Azad, and their contemporaries. At that time, it had emerged as a new style. Hali borrowed words and techniques from English literature and strung them into simple words.

> *Ye diya behtar hai un jhadon aur us lamp se*
> *roshni mahloN ke andar hi rahi jin ki sada*
> *(Altaf Hussain Hali, Nazm: Mitti ka diya)*

> *This earthen lamp is better than the chandelier, and the lamp*
> *whose light was restricted inside the palace and castles*

The poetic works of Azad and Hali were remarkable. However, they were just trendsetters, and the Modern literary movement still had a long way to go. Modernism in Urdu poetry truly surfaced while the progressive writers' movement was in decline, and the experimentation of poets like Meeraji of Halqa-e-Arbab-e-Zauk opened newer avenues. However, Modernist literature took a definitive root in the 1960s.

While the Progressives articulated societal concerns with directness, the Modernists introduced symbolism and stream-of-consciousness writing.

> *Is surmaii roshni meiN rawaN dil ka haara hua kaarvaN hai*
> *charaagh-e-sahar meiN dhuwaN hi dhuwaN hai*
> *(Mazhar Imam)*

> *This grey light hides the defeated caravan of my heart*
> *the morning lamp is full of dark smoke and mist*

The Modernists did not experiment with language alone but dealt with the form and structure of poetry, starting a new trend of anti-ghazal giving birth to *azad ghazal* and *nasri nazm, basri nazm,* and more.

They experimented by intermixing various linguistic tropes, moods, and moments; and playfully transforming words into auditory and visual entities.

> *Sooraj ko choch meiN liye murga khada raha*
> *khidki ke parde kheench diye raat ho gayi*
> *(Nida Fazli)*

> *The cock stands with the sun caught in his beak*
> *I drew the curtains, and it became dark as the night*

Such experiments though eminently forgettable, opened fresh avenues for growth and change in Urdu poetry, and towards the end of Modernism, some excellent poetry emerged.

> *Ek musht-e-khaaq aur wo bhi hawa ki zad meiN hai*
> *zindagi ki bebasi ka istiyaara dekhna*
> *(Parveen Shakir)*

> *A handful of dust and that too is in the control of the breeze*
> *look at this metaphor of helplessness of existence*

However, every movement loses appeal, and its confines become too narrow for the newer generation of writers and poets.

This resulted in the new generation of writers and poets paving their own path and asserting that their writing is not related to any of the established movements — and these became the Post-Modern writers, critics, and poets.

Maa-ba'd Jadidiyat (Post-Modernism)

Post-Modernism was introduced to Urdu literature in the 1980s by Gopi Chand Narang, an eminent scholar and critic of Urdu literature.

Although the experiments that were done with Urdu Nazm, free verse, and blank verse are still prevalent, the Post-Modern poets have restored the structure and form of the classical ghazal. Versification, and eloquence has returned with a fresh and contemporary perspective.

> *Door jitna bhi chala jaaye magar*
> *chaand tujh sa to ho nahi sakta*
> *(Noman Shauque)*

> *Even though it keeps getting far*
> *the moon just can not be as distant as you are*

Post-Modernism does not claim to be a movement, and writers and poets are not expected to follow a particular style.

The evolution of these literary movements gives a good picture of how Urdu poetry has evolved from Mir and Ghalib's time to the present day.

Mir Taqi Mir

Urdu literature is rich with poetic geniuses like Mirza Ghalib, Allama Iqbal, Nazeer Akbarabadi, Mirza Rafi Sauda, Mir Anis, and many more. But Mir Taqi Mir occupies a place that is topmost amongst all the poets of the Urdu language. Mir is *Khuda-e-Sukhan,* the God of poetry. Wallace Stevens, a celebrated American poet, has famously said, "a poet is the priest of the invisible". When a poet puts this invisible into words and makes it visible for all to see, the God of poetry is born.

Mir Mohammad Taqi's birth year was 1722 or 1723 in Akbarabad (Agra) into a family that had migrated from Hejaz in Saudi Arabia to Hindustan two generations prior to his birth. Mir has written a memoir in Persian, a book called *Zikr-e-Mir* in which he talks about his ancestors and early years. This autobiographical account is a bit patchy, not chronological or even complete, but it gives us a fair idea of Mir Taqi Mir's life and times.

Mir's childhood was hugely influenced by his father, Mir Abdullah Ali (Motaqqi), a well-known mystic. He was a *Sufi dervish,* and one can see that this is where the philosophy of Mir's love resides. Mir's uncle Syed Amanullah was also a *dervish* who educated Mir.

In the august company of these two mystics, Mir Taqi Mir grew up, and their teachings influenced the way he looked at the world.

Mir writes that his father often told him that love is supreme and it is on the foundations of love that the world functions. Young as he was, Mir imbibed his father's teachings and practiced them lifelong, making love the primary subject of his poetry.

Mir talks about love with reverence. He may talk of worldly love, of the physical beauty of the beloved, at times even with the frivolousness that comes with youth, but if one looks deeper, one finds that love for him is divinity in all its forms.

> *Parastish ki yaaN tak ki ai but tujhe*
> *nazar mein sabhoN ki khuda kar chale*

> *I idol worshipped you with such strong emotion*
> *and made you God in the world's perception*

Mir's father and uncle were his teachers and his strongest pillars of support. He lost them both within a span of a few months when he was barely eleven years old. Stepbrothers refused to take care of him, and he left for Delhi at the age of 14 years. The events of his growing up, loss of close family members, Delhi's political upheaval, anarchy, and the chaos that followed greatly impacted Mir's impressionable mind. One finds glimpses of agony in his poetry, and the pain that he writes about is not just his; it encompasses the anguish of the entire world.

> *Aah-e-sahar ne sozish-e-dil ko mita diya*
> *Us baav ne hameiN to diya sa bujha diya*

> *A sigh from the dawn and the burning of my heart stopped*
> *extinguished me as if I was a lamp that flickered*

Mir's steadfastness, tenacity, carefree attitude towards material comforts, self-control, and ethics were also the result of his upbringing and the influence his father's ethos had on him. These also get reflected in his poetry. Sufism is about love, and a dervish finds love in everything that surrounds him. This is why Mir's poetry often talks of love and his longing, physical and divine both.

Use dekhuN jidhar ko karuN main nigah
wahi ek soorat hazaroN jagah

Catching my sight wherever I gaze
is that very face at a thousand place

Mir's creative power is extensive. He illustrates his observations from the day-to-day happenings in a simple and easily understood language and creates masterpieces. Look at this *sher* where Mir threads simple words to convey love's insane frenzy.

Koi tum sa bhi kaash tum ko mile
mudd'aa ham ko intekaam se hai

May you find someone just like you
my concern is to get revenge on you

He also uses idioms and phrases from everyday life and threads them into his ashaar splendidly.

Mir amdan bhi koi marta hai
Jaan hai to jahan hai pyare

Who chooses to die wilfully, O! Mir
live and yours will be the world, my dear

and

Munh taka hi kare hai jis tis ka
Hairati hai ye aaina kis ka

It looks expectantly towards any and everyone
Who is the subject of the mirror's admiration?

The era that Mir lived in was when Urdu, or *Rekhta* as it was called back then, was still evolving as a language. Its use in literature was

limited, and people who considered themselves as serious poets and writers preferred using Persian. But Mir chose to use a language that is not laced with flowery Persian words, unlike several of his contemporary poets. His poetry was not for Kings and Nawabs but for the common man. In one couplet, he even declares this.

Sher mere hain sab khawas pasand
par mujhe guftagu aawam se hai

The distinguished find my poetry appealing
but it is with the common man that I prefer conversing

The Persian diction and phraseology had already influenced Rekhta. Mir added the local flavour and used words from *Khadi Boli, Awadhi, Brij Bhasha*, and *Hindustani* to it. He writes *kabhu*, not *kabhi, kisu*, not *kisi* as these were the words used by the common man at that time, thus creating an elegant and natural poetic expression. This style that Mir developed has been used as a guide by several generations of poets that came after Mir.

Dil ki teh ki kahi nahi jaati naazuk hai israar bahut
anchhar haiN to ishq ke do hi, lekin hai bistaar bahut

Can't say how many layers a heart has; it hides delicate secrets
just two magical words of love have a spell that is limitless

Mir's poetry is all-encompassing. He has written on every subject one can think of, and there is one thread - that of love, that binds all of his poetry. *Tasavvuf* (the theology of mysticism) is not forced upon the reader, but on deep analysis, one can find it hiding amongst the simplest of the couplets.

Dikhai diye yuN ki be-khud kiya
hameN aap se bhi juda kar chale

Revealed yourself and intoxicated me
from my own self, you separated me

The subtlety with which Mir conveys his thoughts is something that is rarely found in Urdu poetry. There are thousands of couplets by Mir that demonstrate this unique skill that Mir possessed.

Kehte ho ittehad hai ham ko
haaN kaho aitemaad hai ham ko

You say that you agree with me
will you also say that you have faith in me?

Mir also uses sarcasm very effectively in his poetry. Something one finds in Ghalib's poetry too. But while Ghalib's sarcasm is flirtatious, Mir's sarcasm reveals an ache that is not quite a sharp pain, it is a dull ache which troubles him just enough to express in words.

Shaam se kuch bujha sa rehta hai
dil hua hai chiragh muflis ka

It starts to flicker early in the evening
my heart, it seems is a poor man's lantern

Mir was an egotistical person, as is evident from several anecdotes that are documented. His short temper also made people avoid him. After the catastrophic events in Delhi, he became restless, and then on the invitation of the Nawab Asaf-ud-daula, in 1782, he shifted to Lucknow. Even though he lived in to Lucknow till he died, he did not like the frivolous poetry common in Lucknow those days. He disliked being there but he continued to stay on. However, he never forgot Delhi.

Dil o delhi donoN agar hain kharaba
pai kuch lutf us ujde ghar mein bhi hai

Delhi and my heart even though both are ruined
but pleasure I still find in the remnants of that abode

Mir Taqi Mir lived in Lucknow until he died at 87, on 20th September 1810. His published works are six Diwans that contain 13585 couplets. He has composed poetry in all the poetic forms, including *ghazals, nazm, qita, rubai, masnavi, qaseeda, marsia, na'at, salam, manqaba mukhammas,* etc. His prose works include his autobiography, *Zikr-e-Mir; a* biographical memoir of urdu poets, *Nikat-ul-sho'ra;* and stories about Sufi saints, *Faiz-e-Mir.*

Scholars claim that Mir's *masnavsis* (long narrative poems), *Malumaat-e-Ishq* and *Khwaab-o-khayal,* written in the first person, is an account of Mir's passionate but unsuccessful love affairs and his descent into madness (which he talks about in *Zikr-e-Mir*)

Mir is a master craftsman, and has written mostly about love and yet he is an enigma. While it's not impossible, its very tough to completely understand the poetry of Mir Taqi Mir.

> *Mir Sannah hai milo is se*
> *Dekho to baateN kya banata hai*
>
> *Meet Mir, he is a craftsman,*
> *Look at his expertise in composition*

Mir Taqi Mir

Original painting in colour by Shubnam Gill

Intekhab

صبح تک شمع سر کو دھنتی رہی

کیا پتنگے نے التماس کیا

सुबह तक शमअ' सर को धुनती रही
क्या पतंगे ने इलतेमास किया

Subah tak shama sar ko dhunti rahi
kya patange ne iltemaas kiya

Until morning the flame danced, entranced
wonder what was it that the moth politely asked

دکھ اب فراق کا ہم سے سہا نہیں جاتا
پھر اس پہ ظلم یہ ہے کچھ کہا نہیں جاتا

दुख अब फ़िराक़ का हम से सहा नहीं जाता
फिर उस पे ज़ुल्म ये है कुछ कहा नहीं जाता

Dukh ab firaq ka ham se saha nahiN jaata
phir us pe zulm ye hai kuch kaha nahiN jaata

The pain of your separation I cannot bear anymore
and then this tyranny that I cannot say anything anymore

راہِ دورِ عشق سے روتا ہے کیا
آگے آگے دیکھیے ہوتا ہے کیا

राह-ए-दूर-ए-इश्क़ से रोता है क्या
आगे आगे देखिए होता है क्या

Raah-e-door-e-ishq se rota hai kya
aage aage dekhiye hota hai kya

The path of love is long, and you are lamenting already
keep walking and see what all you will find eventually

دل مجھے اس گلی میں لے جاکر
اور بھی خاک میں ملالایا

दिल मुझे उस गली में ले जा कर
और भी खाक में मिला लाया

Dil mujhe us gali mein le ja kar
aur bhi khaak mein mila laaya

My heart took me to that lane
and made me feel worthless again

افسوس میرے مردے پر اتنا نہ کر کہ اب
پچھتانا یوں ہی سا ہے، جو ہونا تھا ہو چکا

अफसोस मेरे मुर्दें पर इतना न कर कि अब
पछताना यूं ही सा है, जो होना था हो चुका

Afsos mere murde par itna na kar ki ab
pachhtaana yun hi saa hai, jo hona tha ho chuka

Don't grieve on my decrepit remains so much now
repentance is useless, its all in the past now

آنکھوں میں جی مرا ہے ادھر یار دیکھنا
عاشق کا اپنے آخری دیدار دیکھنا

आँखों में जी मिरा है इधर यार देखना
आशिक़ का अपने आखिरी दीदार देखना

AankhoN mein ji mira hai idhar yaar dekhna
aashiq ka apne aakhiri deedar dekhna

Your eyes hold my heart, my beloved, look at me!
glance at your lover, for one last time, look at me!

کام پل میں مرا اتمام کیا
غرض اس شوخ نے بھی کام کیا

काम पल में मिरा तमाम किया
गरज़ उस शोख़ ने भी काम किया

Kaam pal mein mira tamam kiya
garaz us shokh ne bhi kaam kiya

In just a moment my existence she erased
how intentionally the mischievous one worked

ہم نے تو سادگی سے کیا جی کا بھی زیاں

دل جو دیا تھا سو دیا، سر جدا دیا

हम ने तो सादगी से किया जी का भी ज़ियाँ
दिल जो दिया था सो दिया, सर जुदा दिया

Ham ne to saadgi se kiya ji ka bhi ziyaN
dil jo diya tha so diya, sar juda diya

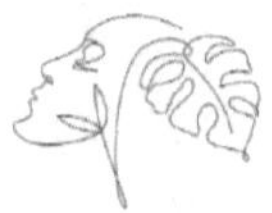

I sacrificed my soul for her in my naivety
along with the heart I also lost my head in modesty

کہتے ہیں آگے تھا بتوں میں بھی رحم
ہے خدا جانیے یہ کب کی بات

कहते हैं आगे था बुतों में भी रहम
है ख़ुदा जानिये यै कब की बात

Kehte hain aage tha butoN mein bhi raham
hai khuda jaaniye ye kab ki baat

They say the idols were full of mercy
God knows when was this actually

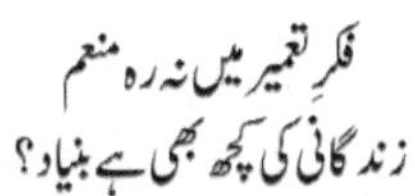

फिक्र-ए-तामीर में न रह मुन'इम
ज़िंदगानी की कुछ भी है बुनियाद ?

Fikr-e-tameer mein na rah mun'im
zindagani ki kuch bhi hai buniyaad?

Don't confer favours in the idea to construct
on its foundation your life is built

جی میں تھا اس سے ملیے تو کیا کیا نہ کہیے میرؔ

پر جب ملے تو رہ گئے ناچار دیکھ کر

जी में था उस से मिलिये तो क्या-क्या न कहिए 'मीर '
पर जब मिले तो रह गए नाचार देख कर

Ji mein tha us se milye to kya kya na kahiye 'Mir'
par jab mile to rah gaye naachaar dekh kar

I wanted to talk my heart out when I meet her
but tongue-tied I became when my sight fell on her

آہ اور اشک ہی سدا ہے یاں
روز برسات کی ہوا ہے یاں

आह और अश्क ही सदा है यां
रोज़ बरसात की हवा है यां

Aah aur ashk hi sada hai yaaN
roz barsaat ki hawa hai yaaN

A sigh and tears are always ready here, on their way
just like the misty breeze is ready here every day

ہم سے کچھ آگے زمانے میں ہوا کیا کیا کچھ
تو بھی ہم غافلوں نے آ کے کیا، کیا کیا کچھ

हम से कुछ आगे ज़माने में हुआ क्या-क्या कुछ
तो भी हम ग़ाफ़िलों ने आ के किया, क्या-क्या कुछ

Ham se aage zamane mein hua kya kya kuch
to bhi ham ghaafiloN ne aa ke kiya, kya kya kuch

In the era just before us transpired, oh! what all!
yet oblivious to it all we kept trying, oh! what all!

رونا یہی ہے مجھ کو تیری جفا سے ہر دم

یہ دل دماغ دونوں کب تک وفا کریں گے

रोना यही है मुझ को तेरी जफ़ा से हर दम
ये दिल दिमाग़ दोनों कब तक वफ़ा करेंगे

Rona yahi hai mujh ko teri jafa se har dam
ye dil dimaagh donoN kab tak wafa kareNge

My lament about your tyranny my beloved, is always this
how long my heart and mind will remain loyal to you

غالب کہ یہ دل خستہ شبِ ہجر میں مر جائے
یہ رات نہی وہ جو کہانی میں گزر جائے

ग़ालिब कि ये दिल-ए-ख़स्ता शब-ए-हिज्र में मर जाये
ये रात नहीं वो जो कहानी में गुज़र जाये

Ghalib ki ye dil-e-khasta shab-e-hijr mein mar jaaye
ye raat nahi wo jo kahani mein guzar jaaye

It is possible my fragile heart in the night of separation
will die
the tale of this night is not such that in one story it will
pass by

غافل تھے ہم احوالِ دلِ خستہ سے اپنے
وہ گنج اسی کنجِ خرابی میں نہاں تھا

ग़ाफ़िल थे हम अहवाल-ए-दिल-ए-ख़स्ता से अपने
वो गंज उसी कुंज-ए-ख़राबी में निहाँ था

Ghafil thae ham ahwal-e-dil-e-khasta se apne
Wo ganj usi kunj-e-kharabi mein nihaN tha

I was unaware of the state of my broken heart because
hidden in a miserable corner that ruined treasure was

عشق میں جی کو صبر و تاب کہاں
اس سے آنکھیں لگیں تو خواب کہاں

इश्क़ में जी को सब्र ओ ताब कहाँ
उस से आँखें लगीं तो ख़्वाब कहाँ

Ishq mein ji ko sabr-o-taab kahaN
us se aankheN lagiN to khwaab kahaN

In love the heart is not patient or tolerant
her one glance makes sleep oh! so distant

گل گئے، بوٹے گئے، گلشن ہوئے برہم گئے
کیسے کیسے ہائے اپنے دیکھتے موسم گئے

गुल गये , बूटे गये , गुलशन हुये बरहम गये
कैसे कैसे हाये अपने देखते मौसम गए

Gul gaye, boote gaye, gulshan huye barham gaye
kaise kaise hai apne dekhte mausam gaye

The flowers, their petals, and the garden are gone,
destroyed
oh! how I saw the seasons passing by, leaving a void

عشق ہمارے خیال پڑا ہے خواب گیا، آرام گیا
جی کا جانا ٹھہر رہا ہے صبح گیا یا شام گیا

इश्क़ हमारे ख़याल पड़ा है, ख़्वाब गया आराम गया
जी का जाना ठहर रहा है, सुबह गया या शाम गया

*Ishq hamare khayal pada hai, khwaab gaya aaram gaya
ji ka jaana thahar raha hai, subah gaya ya shaam gaya*

*In thoughts of love, I have lost my sleep, dreams and
respite
my heart too is waiting to leave, in the moring or at
night*

बहुत की जुस्तजू उस की न पाया
हमें दरपेश है अब जी का खोना

Bahut ki justju us ki na paaya
hameiN darpesh hai ab ji ka khona

Despite my pursuance I could not attain her
I can consider relinquishing my heart now

پتا پتا بوٹا بوٹا حال ہمارا جانے ہے

جانے نہ جانے گل ہی نہ جانے، باغ تو سارا جانے ہے

पत्ता पत्ता बूटा बूटा हाल हमारा जाने है
जाने न जाने गुल ही न जाने, बाग़ तो सारा जाने है

Patta patta boota boota haal hamara jaane hai
jaane na jaane gul hi na jaane, bagh to sara jaane hai

The leaves, plants, and shrubs all know my plight
the garden too is aware, but the flower doesn't know it
quite

کہا میں نے کتنا ہے گل کا ثبات
کلی نے یہ سن کر تبسم کیا

कहा मैं ने कितना है गुल का सबात
कली ने ये सुन कर तबस्सुम किया

Kaha maiN ne kitna hai gul ka sabaat
kali ne ye sun kar tabassum kiya

How long will the flower last, I asked
the flower bud heard me and just smiled

دل وہ نگر نہیں کہ پھر آباد ہو سکے
پچھتاؤ گے ، سنو ہو؟ یہ بستی اُجاڑ کر

दिल वो नगर नहीं कि फिर आबाद हो सके
पछताओगे सुनो हो? ये बस्ती उजाड़ कर

Dil wo nagar nahiN ki phir aabaad ho sake
pachhtaoge suno ho? Ye basti ujaad kar

My heart is not a city that can be inhabited anew
listen to me, if you ruin this hamlet, you will rue

اب دیکھ لے کہ سینہ بھی تازہ ہوا ہے چاک
پھر ہم سے اپنا حال دکھایا نہ جائے گا

अब देख ले कि सीना भी ताज़ा हुआ है चाक
फिर हम से अपना हाल दिखाया न जाएगा

Ab dekh le ki seena bhi taaza hua hai chaak
phir ham se apna haal dikhaya na jayega

Look at my chest that has just been cut open
I won't be in the state to show it to you again

نہ دیکھا میر آوارہ کو لیکن
غبار اک ناتواں سا کو بہ کو تھا

न देखा 'मीर' आवारा को लेकिन
ग़ुबार इक नातवाँ सा कू-ब-कू था

Na dekha 'Mir' aawara ko lekin
ghubar ik naatavaN sa ku-ba-ku tha

I have not seen 'Mir' the vagabond, however
there was a faint dust cloud everywhere

میرے رونے کی حقیقت جس میں تھی
ایک مدت تک وہ کاغز نم رہا

मेरे रोने की हक़ीक़त जिस में थी
एक मुद्दत तक वो काग़ज़ नम रहा

Mere rone ki haqeeqat jis meiN thi
ek muddat tak wo kaghaz nam raha

Narrating the truth of my tear-filled eyes
the paper was moist for a long while

عشق اک میرؔ بھاری پتھر ہے
کب یہ تجھ ناتواں سے اٹھتا ہے

इश्क़ इक 'मीर' भारी पत्थर है
कब ये तुझ नातवाँ से उठता है

Ishq ik 'Mir' bhari patthar hai
kab ye tujh na-tavaN se uth-ta hai

Love, 'Mir', is burdensome like a heavy stone
how will you lift it? You are a frail-bodied one

وہ تو کل دیر تلک دیکھتا اُدھر کو رہا
ہم سے ہی حالِ تباہ اپنا دکھایا نہ گیا

वो तो कल देर तलक देखता इधर को रहा
हम से ही हाल-ए-तबाह अपना दिखाया न गया

*Wo to kal der talak dekhta idhar ko raha
ham se hi haal-e-tabah apna dikhaya na gaya*

*Although they kept looking at me for a very long time
I could not bring myself to show them this sorry state of
mine*

مشکل ہے مٹ گئے نقشوں کی پھر نمود

جو صورتیں بگڑ گئیں ان کا نہ کر خیال

मुश्किल है मिट गए नक़्शों की फिर नुमूद
जो सूरतें बिगड़ गईं उन का न कर ख़याल

Mushkil hai mit gaye naqshoN ki phir numud
jo soorteN bigad gayiN un ka na kar khayaal

It is tough for the erased imprints to reappear, you see
the fate that is destroyed, don't imagine it to be

کچھ کرو فکر مجھ دِوانے کی
دھوم ہے پھر بہار آنے کی

कुछ करो फिक्र मुझ दिवाने की
धूम है फिर बहार आने की

Kuch karo fikr mujh diwane ki
dhoom hai phir bahaar aane ki

Have some concern for this lunatic lover
spring is arriving again in all its grandeur

کوشش اپنی تھی عبث، پر کی بہت

کیا کریں ہم، چاہتا تھا جی بہت

कोशिश अपनी थी अबस, पर की बहुत
क्या करें हम, चाहता था जी बहुत

Koshish apni thi abas, par ki bahut
kya kareN ham, chahta tha ji bahut

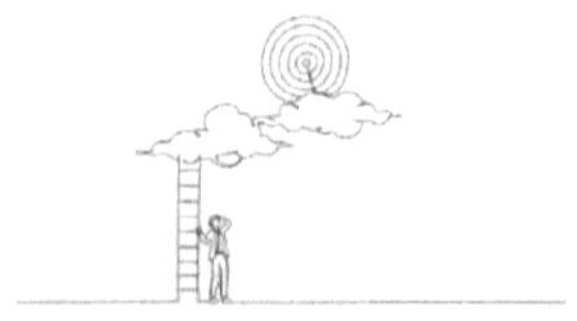

My efforts were futile, but I worked relentlessly
what could I do? My heart wanted it immensely

بات کہتے جی کا جانا ہو گیا
مرنا عاشق کا بہانا ہو گیا

बात कहते जी का जाना हो गया
मरना आशिक़ का बहाना हो गया

Baat kehte ji ka jaana ho gaya
marna aashiq ka bahana ho gaya

His heartbeat ceased after he voiced his thoughts
it became an excuse for the lover's demise

آنے کے وقت تم تو کہیں کے کہیں رہے

اب آئے تم، فائدہ؟ ہم ہی نہیں رہے

आने के वक़्त तुम तो कहीं के कहीं रहे

अब आए तुम, फ़ायदा? हम ही नहीं रहे

Aane ke waqt tum to kahiN ke kahiN rahe
ab aaye tum, fayeda?ham hi nahiN rahe

When it was the time to come, you were nowhere to be
found
what's the point in coming now, when I am not around

دنیا میں کوئی پھر پھر آیا نہیں ہے صاحب
اک بار تم کو مرنا ہی میرؔ ہے مناسب

दुनिया में कोई फिर फिर आया नहीं है साहब
इक बार तुम को मरना ही मीर है मुनासिब

Dunia mein koi phir phir aaya nahiN hai saheb
ek baar tum ko marna hi Mir hai munasib

No one comes back in this world, my friend
one day for you too, 'Mir', death will be the only proper
end

عشق ہمارا آہ نہ پوچھو کیا کیا رنگ بدلتا ہے
خون ہوا دل، داغ ہوا، پھر درد ہوا، پھر غم ہے اب

इश्क़ हमारा आह न पूछो क्या-क्या रंग बदलता है
ख़ून हुआ दिल, दाग़ हुआ, फिर दर्द हुआ, फिर ग़म है अब

*Ishq hamara aah na poocho kya kya rang badalta hai
khoon hua dil, daagh hua, phir dard hua, phir gham hai ab*

*Oh! Do not ask me how my love keeps changing colours
my heart bleeds, it scars, then aches, and now it mourns*

ہستی اپنی حباب کی سی ہے
یہ نمائش سراب کی سی ہے

हस्ती अपनी हुबाब की सी है
ये नुमाइश सराब की सी है

Hasti apni hubaab ki si hai
ye numaaish saraab ki si hai

This life is nothing but a bubble, its ephemeral
a mirage, all this show, it is evasive and unreliable

مگر دیوانہ تھا گل بھی کسو کا
کہ پیراہن میں سو جاگا رفو تھا

मगर दीवाना था गुल भी किसू का
कि पैराहन में सौ जागा रफ़ू था

Magar deewana tha gul bhi kisu ka
ki pairahan mein sau jaaga rafu tha

But the flower too was enamoured with someone
for, his garment had hundered of mendings done

کیا ہے گلشن میں جو قفس میں نہیں
عاشقوں کا جلا وطن دیکھا

क्या है गुलशन में जो क़फ़स में नहीं
आशिक़ों का जिला-वतन देखा

Kya hai gulshan mein jo qafas mein nahiN
aashiqon ka jila-watan dekha

Isn't a garden same as the prison?
I have seen the lovers in exile here

جو اس شور سے میر روتا رہے گا
تو ہم سایہ کاہے کو سو تا رہے گا

जो इस शोर से 'मीर' रोता रहेगा
तो हम साया काहे को सोता रहेगा

Jo is shor se 'Mir' rota rahega
to ham-saaya kahe ko sota rahega

'Mir' if you so loudly keep weeping
then how can your neighbour keep sleeping

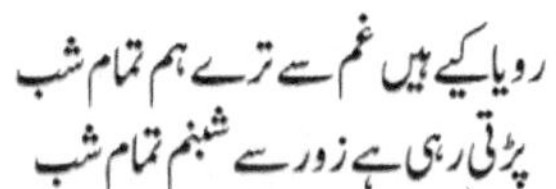

रोया किये हैं ग़म से तिरे हम तमाम शब
पड़ती रही है ज़ोर से शबनम तमाम शब

Roya kiye haiN gham se tire ham tamam shab
padti rahi hai zor se shabnam tamam shab

Grieving for you, I was crying all night
causing the dew to keep falling all night

آتشِ دل نہیں بجھی شاید
قطرۂ اشک ہے شرارہ ہنوز

आतिश-ए-दिल नहीं बुझी शायद
क़तरा-ए-अश्क है शरारा हनूज़

Aatish-e-dil nahiN bujhi shayad
Qatra-e-ashq hai sharara hanuz

The fire in my heart hasn't been extinguished perhaps
there are still some sparks in my teardrops

باقی یہ داستان ہے اور کل کی رات ہے
گر جان میری میؔر نہ آ پہنچے لب تلک

बाक़ी ये दास्तान है और कल की रात है
गर जान मेरी 'मीर' न आ पहुंचे लब तलक

Baqi ye daastan hai aur kal ki raat hai
Gar jaan meri 'Mir' na aa pahunche lab talak

This story is incomplete, and there is one more night
If by then 'Mir' is spared his life, and he is alright

بے کلی، بے خودی کچھ آج نہیں
ایک مّدت سے وہ مزاج نہیں

बेकली, बेख़ुदी कुछ आज नहीं
एक मुद्दत से वो मिज़ाज नहीं

Be-kali, bekhudi kuch aaj nahiN
ek muddat se wo mizaaj nahiN

Restlessness, intoxication, nothing today
it's been a while since that temperament went away

ہم آپ ہی کو اپنا مقصود جانتے ہیں
اپنے سوائے کس کو موجود جانتے ہیں

हम आप ही को अपना मक़सूद जानते हैं
अपने सिवाये किस को मौजूद जानते हैं

Ham aap hi ko apne maqsood jaante haiN
apne siwaye kis ko maujood jaante haiN

I cherish myself, and that is all I understand
I am the only one who exists, that is all I understand

مر کر بھی ہاتھ اوے تو میؔ مفت ہے وہ
جی کے زیان کو بھی ہم سود جانتے ہیں

मर कर भी हाथ आवे तो 'मीर' मुफ़्त है वो
जी के ज़ियान को भी हम सूद जानते हैं

Mar kar bhi haath aawe to 'Mir' muft hai wo
ji ke ziyaan ko bhi ham sood jaante haiN

If death can bring her, 'Mir' life can be freely laid
loss of heart to her will be just an interest paid

حرم کو جائے یا دیر میں بسر کرے
تری تلاش میں اک دل کدھر کدھر کرے

हरम को जाये या दैर में बसर करे
तिरी तलाश में इक दिल किधर किधर करे

Haram ko jaye ya dair mein basar kare
tiri talash mein ik dil kidhar kidhar kare

Vist Mecca or go to a temple and perch
where all will this one heart go in your search

وہ کیا چیز ہے آہ جس کے لیے
ہر اک چیز سے دل اٹھا کر چلے

वो क्या चीज़ है आह जिस के लिए
हर इक चीज़ से दिल उठा कर चले

Wo kya cheez hai aah jis ke liye
har ik cheez se dil utha kar chale

Ah! what is that thing that could make
my heart to lose interest, and to forsake

کل تک تو ہم پے ہنستے چلے آئے تھے یہیں
مرنا بھی میر جی کا تماشا سا ہو گیا

कल तक तो हम पे हँसते चले आए थे यहीं
मरना भी मीर जी का तमाशा सा हो गया

Kal tak to ham pe hanste chale aaye the yahiN
marna bhi Mir ji ka tamasha sa ho gaya

For all those who made fun of me till yesterday
'Mir's death too has become an amusement today

اس سے یوں گل نے رنگ پکڑا ہے
شمع سے جیسے لیں چراغ لگا

उस से यूं गुल ने रंग पकड़ा है
शमा से जैसे लें चिराग़ लगा

Us se yun gul ne rang pakda hai
shama se jaise leN chiragh laga

From her colours the flower borrows its pigment
like the candle flame lights a lamp brilliant

دل گیا مفت اور د کھ پایا
ہو کے عاشق بہت میں پچھتایا

दिल गया मुफ़्त और दुख पाया
हो के आशिक़ बहुत मैं पछताया

Dil gaya muft aur dukh paaya
ho ke aashiq bahut main pachhtaaya

I lost my heart and gained misery for no cost
by becoming her lover, I repented a lot

Forms and structure of Urdu poetry

Traditional Urdu poetry has several forms, the most commonly known are *ghazal* and *nazm*.

Nazm is one of the most significant genres of Urdu poetry and is extremely popular. Urdu poets have written nazms on various topics, including philosophy, politics, the day-to-day life of ordinary folks, festivals, and more. The classical *nazm* is written in rhymed verse. However, the modern nazm has evolved to include free verse and spoken poetry. A *nazm* is a form of descriptive poetry and can be short or long, and there are no restrictions on its rhyming scheme. *Hamd, Na'at, Manqabat, Marsia, Masnavi, Qasida,* and *Rubaii* are also forms of Nazm.

Hamd is poetry written in praise of the Almighty, and *Na'at* praises the Islamic prophet, Muhammad. *Manqabat* is a Sufi devotional poem. *Marsia* is elegiac poetry of mourning written when someone close and much-loved dies. The classical Marsia in Urdu poetry laments the martyrdom of Imam Hussain and his companions in the battle of Karbala. A *Qasida* is written as an ode to a benefactor and it can also be satirical. *Masnavi* is a long poem often narrating stories and historical events, and *Tazkira* is a biographical anthology of poetry.

Rubaii is a four-line verse with its own, and unique rhyming structure whereas a *Qita* is a four-line verse that follows the norms of ghazal

Ghazal is the other very popular genre and significant to Urdu poetry. The Urdu ghazal originated as a form of an amatory poem that consisted of rhyming couplets called Ashaar. (a single couplet is called a Sher, its plural is ashaar)

The couplets of a *ghazal*, unlike those of a *nazm*, do not require a common theme. Each sher of a ghazal holds the entire expression of a thought and is self-contained and distinct from the others. They are, however, bound together by a thematic or tonal connotation.

A poem to be called a Ghazal should follow a set of rules. It has a collection of ashaar, and each sher of a ghazal can be enjoyed, interpreted, and quoted independently.

Sher or a couplet is a small poem in itself. Each line of this couplet is called a m*isra*. The first line, *misra-e-ula*, is a statement, and the second line, *misra-e-sani*, qualifies, describes, elaborates, or justifies the first Misra.

Koi ummeed bar nahi aati
koi soorat nazar nahi aati

Maut ka ek din muyyan hai
neend kyon raat bhar nahi aati

In this sher, 'koi ummeed bar nahi aati' is misra-e-ula, and 'koi soorat nazar nahi aati' is misra-e-sani.

Every sher of a ghazal has a rhyme and a refrain. These are called *qafiyaa* and *radif.*

Radiif can be a word or a phrase. In the sher above, the radiif is 'nahi aati'. A ghazal contains just one radiif, and the second line of each couplet of the Ghazal must end on this radiif.

Qafiyaa is the rhyming pattern preceding the Radiif, which must be consistent throughout the Ghazal. The Qafiyaa can be a letter or a word. For example, in the above ashaar, the Qawafii are - bar, *nazar, and bhar*.

Matlaa is the first sher of a ghazal, and it must have the Radiif and Qafiyaa in both lines of the couplet.

Maqta is a sher with the poet's takhallus or *nom de plume*. It is typically the last sher of a ghazal and is more personal. The poets are skillful in weaving the meanings of their takhallus in the sher, thereby giving additional layers of meaning to the couplet.

Kaaba kis munh se jaoge 'Ghalib'
sharm tum ko magar nahi aati

Bah'r / Vazn Ghazals follow a set meter and syllabic count, and all the ashaar in a ghazal follow the pattern. The *bah'r* is a pattern that combines the syllabic counts of Urdu parody, determining the length or *vazan* of a ghazal. There are 32 types of *bah'r*, out of which 19 are commonly used. It is a complex system of syllabic rhyming, so for ease of understanding, the *bah'r* is roughly classified into three types: short, medium, and long.

This sher is an example of a short b*ah'r:*

Dil-e-naadaN tujhe hua kya hai
aakhir is dard ki dawaa kya hai

This is an example of medium *bah'r:*

Umr jalvoN meiN basar ho ye zaroori to nahiN
har shab-e-gham ki sahar ho ye zaroori to nahiN

And, this is an example of a *long bah'r:*

Ae mere hamnashiN chal kahiN aur chal, is chaman meiN ab apna guzaara nahiN
baat hoti guloN ki to sah lete ham, ab to kaatoN pe bhi haq hamaraa nahiN

Over the years, *ghazal* has evolved in terms of vocabulary and phrasings, enabling it to reach a wider audience. Contemporary poets are also more relaxed about the conventions and standards of Ghazal

Books in this series

- Mirza Ghalib

- Mir Taqi Mir

- Firaq Gorakhpuri

- Seemab Akbarabadi

- Faiz Ahmad Faiz

- Sahir Ludhianvi

- Meeraji

- Parvin Shakir

Author contact: swatisani@gmail.com

www.ingramcontent.com/pod-product-compliance
Lightning Source LLC
Chambersburg PA
CBHW051447140726
47987CB00006B/2574